A Net, a Cup, and a Bug

Illustrated by Karen Bell

High-Frequency Words

a   the   with   said   to   was   of

Scott Foresman

Editorial Offices: Glenview, Illinois • Parsippany, New Jersey • New York, New York
Sales Offices: Parsippany, New Jersey • Duluth, Georgia • Glenview, Illinois
Coppell, Texas • Ontario, California

Diz and Sam sat in the sand.

Sam had a net.

Diz had a big cup with a lid.

Sam said to get up fast!

A bug was on Diz.

A big bug was on top of Diz.

Will Diz get the bug
with the cup?

Will Sam get the bug
with the net?

Bam! Bump! Bop!

Bump! Bop!

Diz and Sam sat in the sand.

Diz had a net.

Sam had a big cup with a lid.